Withdrawn

The Cajun
Cornbread Boy

The Cajun Cornbread Boy

A Well-Loved Tale Spiced Up by Dianne de Las Casas
Illustrated by Marita Gentry

PELICAN PUBLISHING COMPANY
Gretna 2009

For Soleil and Eliana, who spice up my life—D. d. L. C.

For Dianne, who never stops running!—M. G.

Copyright © 2009
By Dianne de Las Casas

Illustrations copyright © 2009
By Marita Gentry

---

*The word "Pelican" and the depiction of a pelican
are trademarks of Pelican Publishing Company, Inc.,
and are registered in the U.S. Patent and Trademark Office.*

Library of Congress Cataloging-in-Publication Data

De las Casas, Dianne.
  The Cajun cornbread boy : a well-loved tale spiced up / by Dianne de Las Casas ;
illustrated by Marita Gentry.
      p. cm.
  Summary: A freshly baked cornbread boy escapes when he is taken out of the oven
and eludes a number of hungry animals as well as having a spicy encounter with an
alligator in this Cajun version of the Gingerbread boy.
  ISBN 978-1-58980-224-7 (hardcover : alk. paper) [1. Fairy tales. 2. Corn bread—
Fiction. 3. Alligators—Fiction. 4. Cajuns—Fiction.] I. Gentry, Marita, ill. II. Title.
  PZ8.D3735Caj 2009
  [E]—dc22

                                                            2008030439

Printed in Singapore
Published by Pelican Publishing Company, Inc.
1000 Burmaster Street, Gretna, Louisiana 70053

THE CAJUN CORNBREAD BOY

Down by the bayou, there lived an old Cajun
woman who had no children. More than anything,
she wanted a child.

One day, she decided to make a cornbread boy.
She put the ingredients into a bowl, adding a
little bit of this and a little bit of that and a *big*
dash of cayenne pepper.

Finally, she poured the batter into a black iron skillet. She said, "My *grand-mère* used this old skillet often to make magic cornbread. It should do the trick!" On top of the batter, she added two chilies for the eyes, a peppercorn for the nose, and a link of boudin for the mouth. Mmm, mmm, mmm! She placed the cornbread boy into the oven, and soon he was done.

When the old woman opened the oven, she added two pats of butter for the cheeks. But surprise, surprise!

That round cornbread boy sprouted arms and legs, jumped up, and ran out the front door. He cried:

"Run, *chère*, run, as fast as you can!
You can't catch me—I'm full of cayenne."

The Cajun cornbread boy ran into the woods.

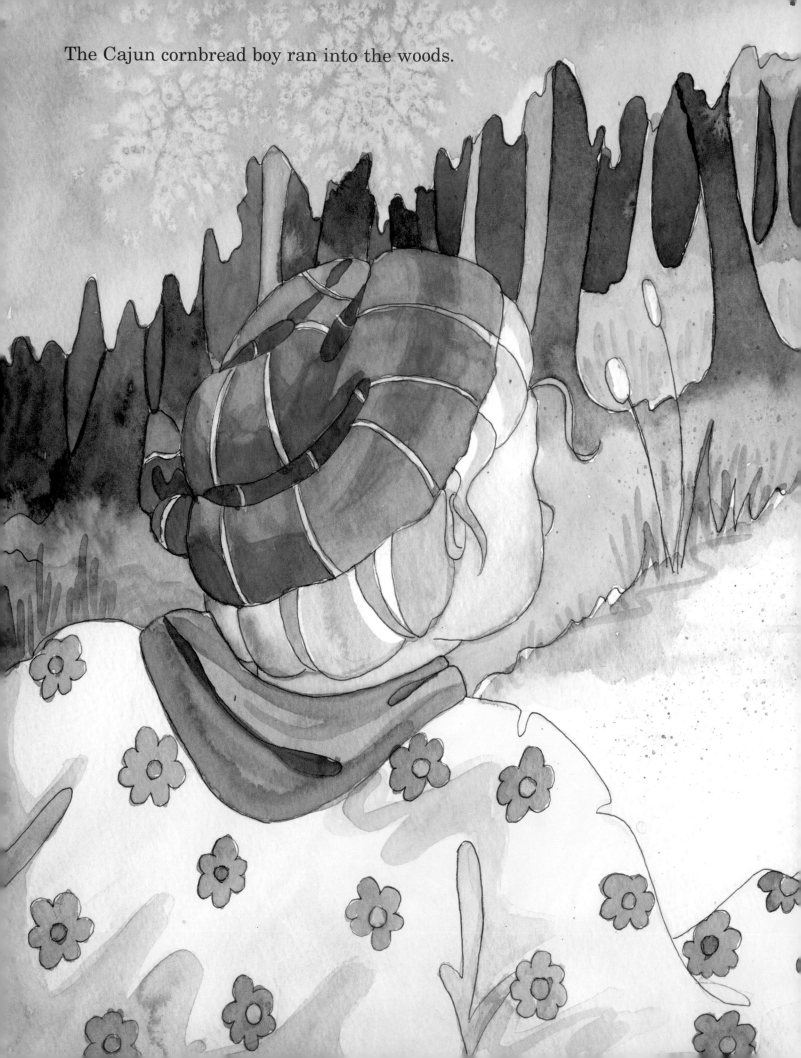

The old woman began chasing him with a jump, a skip, and a hop, yelling, "Please stop, Cornbread Boy, stop!" But the Cajun cornbread boy sprinted away.

Soon he came upon a rascally raccoon.

The raccoon eyed the cornbread boy hungrily and asked, "Won't you stop, Cornbread Boy? I'd love to have you for breakfast."

• But the Cajun cornbread boy did not stop. He kept running, crying out:

"Run, *cher,* run, as fast as you can!
You can't catch me—I'm full of cayenne."

The raccoon began chasing him with a jump, a skip, and a hop, yelling, "Please stop, Cornbread Boy, stop!" But the Cajun cornbread boy sprinted away.

The Cajun cornbread boy ran deeper into the woods. Next, he came upon a fierce fox.

The fox eyed the cornbread boy hungrily and asked, "Won't you stop, Cornbread Boy? I'd love to have you for lunch."

But the Cajun cornbread boy did not stop. He kept running, crying out:
"Run, *cher*, run, as fast as you can!
You can't catch me—I'm full of cayenne."

The fox began chasing him with a jump, a skip, and a hop, yelling, "Please stop, Cornbread Boy, stop!" But the Cajun cornbread boy sprinted away.

The Cajun cornbread boy ran until he came to the bayou. He wanted to cross the water to get away from the fox, but he could not. He didn't know how to swim. By and by, an artful alligator swam to the shore.

"*Bonjour*, Cornbread Boy. Are you crossing the bayou?"

"I can't swim. How will I get across?" asked the cornbread boy.

"Well," said the alligator slyly, "I could swim you across, and once we get to the other side, I'd love to have you for dinner." The gator gave a big, toothy grin.

"For sure," said the Cajun cornbread boy. So he hopped onto Gator's back, and they began to cross the bayou. As they went farther across the bayou, the water got deeper and deeper and deeper! The Cajun cornbread boy had to move farther and farther up Gator's back, until he was finally on Gator's snout.

When they neared the opposite bank, Gator jumped up, sending the cornbread boy flying into the air and into Gator's mouth.

But something funny happened, *mes amis*.
That cornbread boy was so spicy he set Gator's
tongue on fire! Gator spit him out and swam
away lickety-split.

The Cajuns down by the bayou say that they still see that gator swimming around with his mouth wide open, fanning himself. Gator sure learned his lesson. Playing tricks can backfire. You can bet he won't be eating any more spicy Cajun cornbread!

As for the Cajun cornbread boy, to this day, you can still hear him singing:
"Run, *cher*, run, as fast as you can!
You can't catch me—I'm full of cayenne."

Southern Cornbread

4 tbsp. bacon drippings or vegetable oil
2 cups self-rising cornmeal
2 eggs, beaten
2 cups buttermilk

Heat oven to 450 degrees. Grease a cast-iron skillet with 2 tbsp. drippings or oil, coating entire pan and leaving remainder at bottom. Heat skillet in oven.

Mix cornmeal, eggs, buttermilk, and 2 tbsp. drippings. Pour batter into hot skillet. Bake for 35 minutes or until golden brown. Cut into 6-8 wedges.

Note: If you sprinkle a little cornmeal in hot pan before adding batter, it will add a crispier texture.

Optional: To spice it up, add a dash cayenne pepper to batter. Ooh yeah, *cher!*

Glossary

artful: sly, cunning

bonjour (bone-ZHOOR): French for "hello"

boudin (BOO-dan): delicious Cajun sausage made of rice and meat

cayenne (KIE-yen): spicy pepper that is ground into a powder and used to flavor food

cher (sha): French for "dear" (when speaking to a man or boy)

chère (shair): French for "dear" (when speaking to a woman or girl)

grand-mère (gron-MAIR): French for "grandmother"

mes amis (mayz ah-MEE): French for "my friends"

rascally: mischievous

Author's Note

This story was adapted from my childhood memories of "The Gingerbread Boy." A United States version called "Journey Cake, Ho!," which is a variant of a European folktale, can be found in *The Arbuthnot Anthology of Children's Literature,* Third Edition (Glenview, Ill., 1971). I added a spicy twist to the end of the story because the Cajun Cornbread Boy is, after all, full of cayenne and much too hot to eat.